AF483842

IT STARTS WITH HELLO

KATIE'S STORY   ABOUT PRADER-WILLI SYNDROME

BY: DESTINY PACHA, ED.D.
ILLUSTRATED BY: TARA ESPINOSA BRADLEY

To my unicorn, you know who you are. —D.P.

214
MAIL

Hello! My name is Katie! I live with my mom, dad, big brother, and my two dogs. I have Prader-Willi syndrome, which is a rare disorder I was born with. I have been told I am so rare, I am like a unicorn!

Everyone is a little bit different, which makes us all special. Maybe you are left handed or wear glasses. Maybe you like the color brown, but your friend likes blue. Or maybe you speak a different language or use pictures to communicate.

WHAT MAKES YOU DIFFERENT AND SPECIAL?

Daily
Schedule
Morning:
• make bed
• brush teeth
• feed fishy
Night:
• clean room
• brush teeth
• put on pjs

4

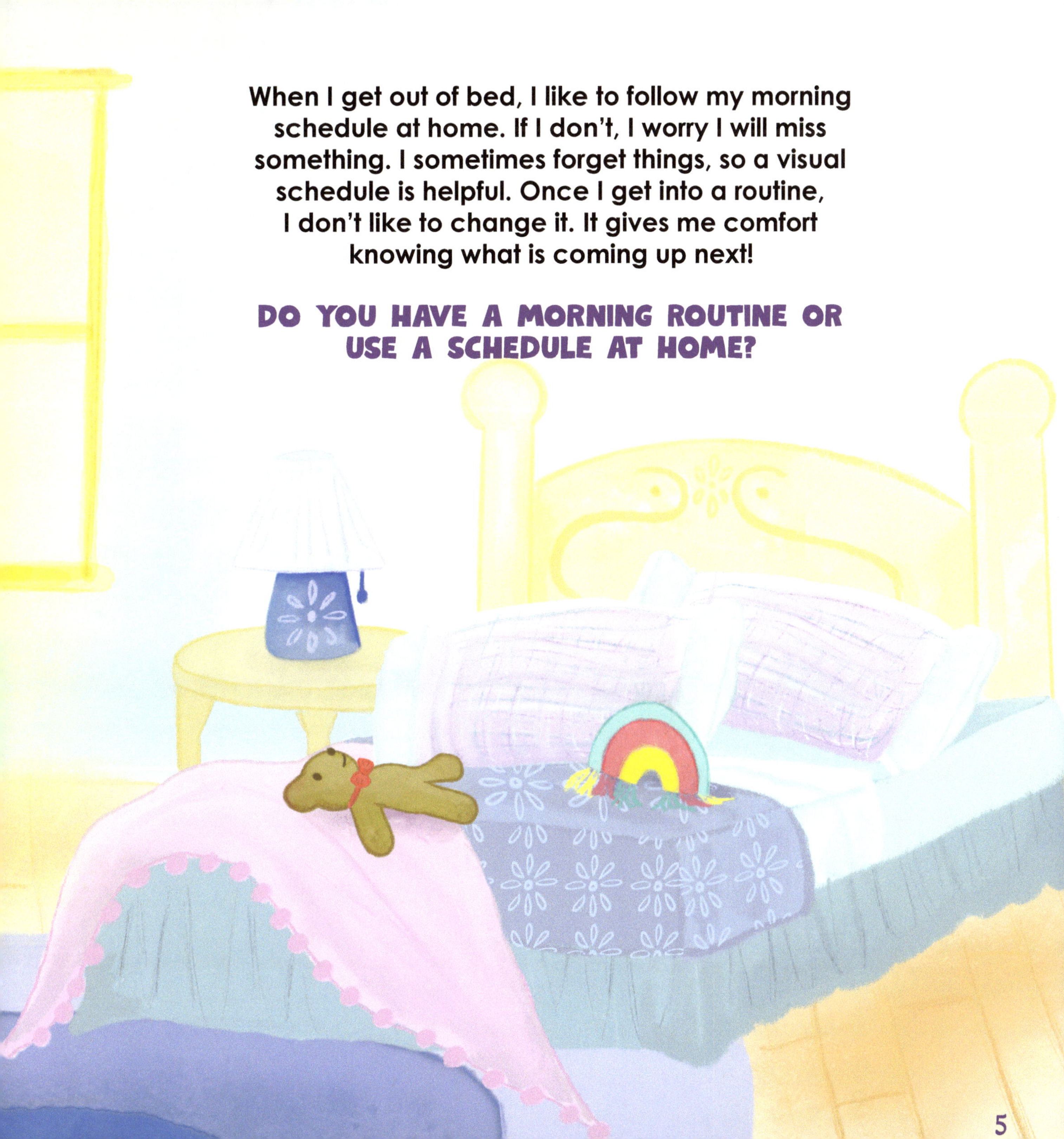

When I get out of bed, I like to follow my morning schedule at home. If I don't, I worry I will miss something. I sometimes forget things, so a visual schedule is helpful. Once I get into a routine, I don't like to change it. It gives me comfort knowing what is coming up next!

DO YOU HAVE A MORNING ROUTINE OR USE A SCHEDULE AT HOME?

There are so many exciting things around me. I am easily distracted, so I usually need help getting to class with an adult. To keep me focused on my work, I like to know what is next, so I have a *First and Then* board on my desk, and get regular reminders from my teacher.

DO YOU EVER GET DISTRACTED WHEN YOU ARE GOING SOMEWHERE, OR NEED REMINDERS TO FINISH YOUR WORK?

12 - 8 =
Today's Schedule
8:45-9:15 Morning Meeting
9:15-10:15 Reading
10:15-11:00 Art/Music
11:00-12:00 Math
12:00-12:45 Lunch/Recess
12:45-1:15 Writing/Spelling
1:15-2:00 Science
2:00-2:30 Centers
2:30 Pack-up/Dismissal
FIRST THEN
MATH LUNCH
9-4
12-8=
Name: Katie

KATIE

You may notice I eat at the same time every day, and only specific food from home. I usually have whole grains, healthy proteins, some fruit, and lots of vegetables for lunch. Sweets and other snacks in your lunch can make me sick, so please don't share with me. If I eat something I shouldn't, it is very important for an adult to know so they can keep me safe.

DO YOU BRING YOUR LUNCH TO SCHOOL OR DO YOU GET IT FROM THE CAFETERIA?

Although I want to run and play, my body gets tired easily and I can get too hot (or too cold) outside without knowing it. That's why I might need to take a break or even rest after recess. The muscles in my body are not as strong as yours and I sometimes lose my balance. I may need help from an adult to climb stairs or play on the playground, but that doesn't stop me from having fun!

AFTER RUNNING AND PLAYING, DO YOU EVER NEED TO TAKE A BREAK?

Nurse ♥ + Dawn

When I get a bug bite or a small cut, I
sometimes scratch it too much, so I may
need to go see the nurse to put a Band-Aid® on it.
The Band-Aids® help me not scratch and keep
me safe. Nurse Dawn also helps me when
my belly hurts or if I fall down.

**DO BUG BITES ITCH YOU, TOO? HAVE
YOU EVER NEEDED A BAND-AID® OR
SEEN A NURSE? I THINK ALL KIDS HAVE.**

Change is difficult for me! I don't like it when something is going to be different in my day. I really like routines! It is helpful if I am given a warning before, but I may still have lots of questions. I don't mean to be a bother, I just want to make sure I know what to expect.

Z
is for
Zebra
CHANGE CAN BE DIFFICULT FOR A LOT OF KIDS. DO YOU EVER GET WORRIED WHEN YOU DON'T KNOW WHAT IS GOING TO HAPPEN NEXT?
Today's Schedule
8:45-9:15 Morning Meeting
9:15-10:15 Reading
10:15-11:00 Art/Music
11:00-12:00 Math
12:00-12:45 Lunch/Recess
12:45-1:15 Writing/Spelling
1:15-2:00 Science
2:00-2:30 Centers
2:30 Pack-up/Dismissal
SCHEDULE CHANGE

CALM CORNER

If I start to get upset, it's best for me to have space and time to think. If I need to calm down, I may go to a quiet corner and play with puzzles or fidgets.

WHEN YOU GET UPSET, WHAT KIND OF ACTIVITIES OR TOYS HELP YOU CALM DOWN?

When someone asks me a question, I might not respond right away. I often need to think and make sure I understand before I answer. Too many questions at once can confuse me, and I might need reminders from an adult about what I should do next.

WHAT KINDS OF THINGS DO YOU NEED EXTRA TIME TO THINK ABOUT? DO YOU EVER NEED A REMINDER TO FINISH WORK OR A TASK?

Sometimes phrases can confuse me, especially when they don't match what they mean. I am learning about these types of sayings, and might need help understanding some jokes!

DID YOU KNOW THAT WHEN SOMEONE SAYS, "IT IS RAINING CATS AND DOGS," IT REALLY MEANS THAT IT IS RAINING A LOT OUTSIDE? DO YOU KNOW OTHER SAYINGS LIKE THIS?

Get out of here! You are really good at this!
No! I am not going anywhere. That is mean. I don't want to play with you anymore.
Holiday Stuff
Birthday supplies

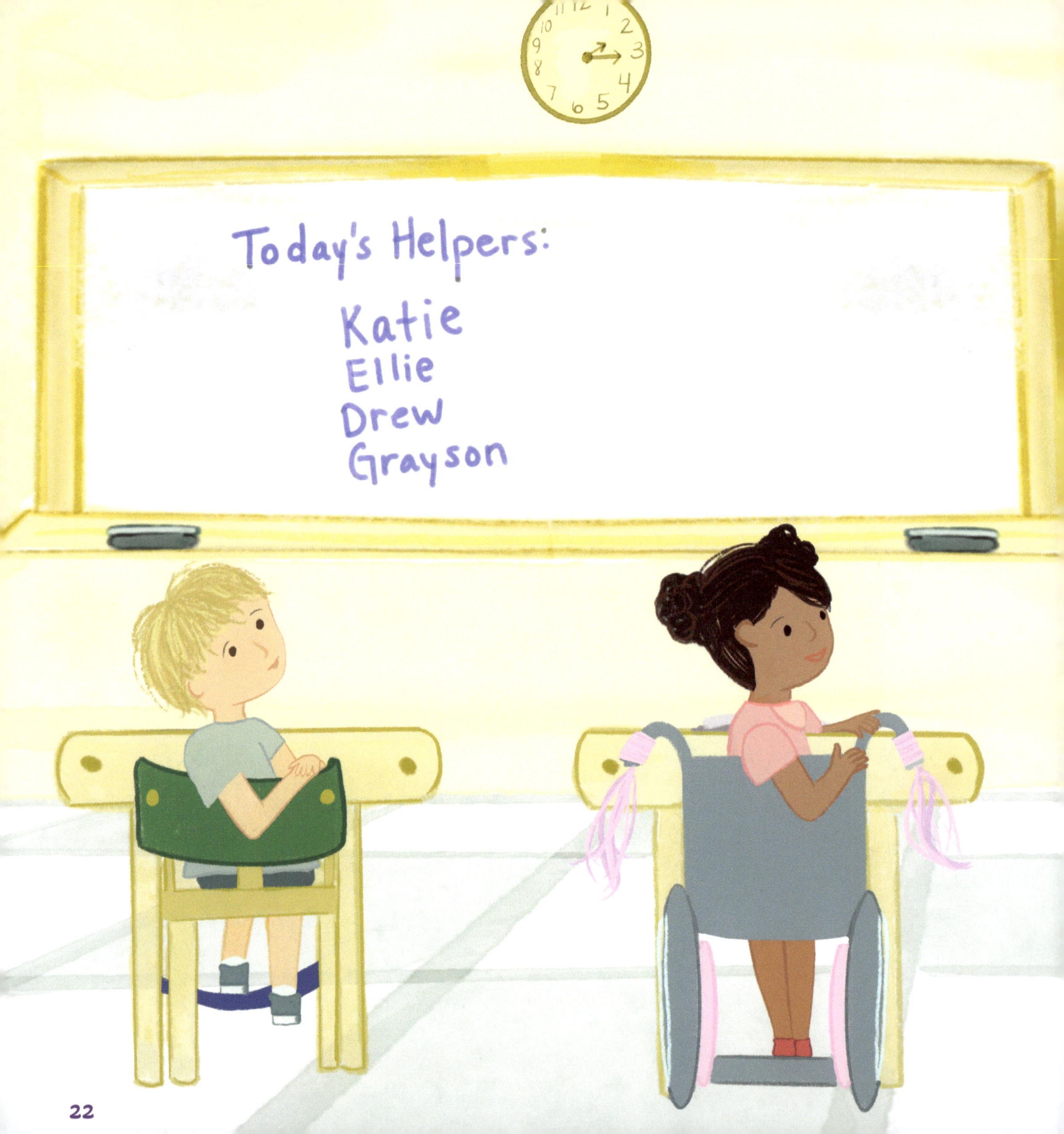

22

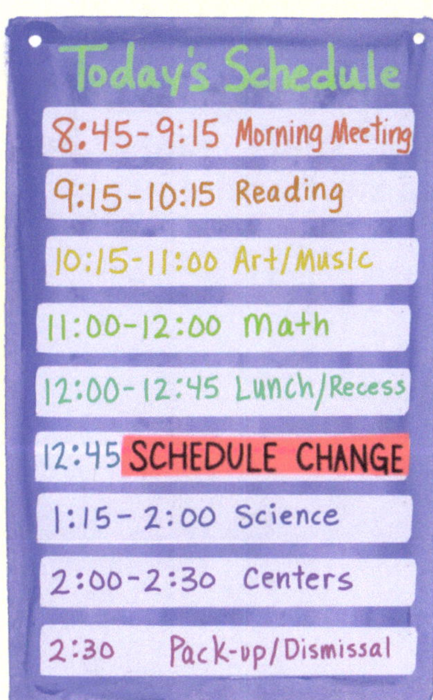

I have a kind heart and I love to help my teachers and friends. I always volunteer to be a helper, it is one of my favorite things to do!

DO YOU LIKE TO HELP OTHERS? DOES IT MAKE YOUR HEART HAPPY, LIKE IT DOES MINE?

Even though I have Prader-Willi syndrome and may do some things a little differently, we are still a lot alike. I may be rare, but I don't care. I am just a kid and I want to be your friend, and that starts with hello!

LET'S GO PLAY!

FOR THE MOST COMPREHENSIVE INFORMATION
ON PRADER-WILLI SYNDROME (PWS),
PLEASE REFER TO THESE EXPERTS:

FOR A FREE GROWN-UP READING GUIDE,
WITH DETAILED EXPLANATION OF KATIE'S PWS
TRAITS AND PRINTABLE EDUCATIONAL RESOURCES,
VISIT EMPOWEREDSOLUTIONS.ORG

ABOUT THE AUTHOR

Dr. Destiny Pacha is a PWS Education Specialist with over 20 years of experience in the education field. She focuses on supporting families by working with school personnel to understand the educational implications of PWS. She also provides consultation services on assessing and implementing procedures to create a food-secure educational environment. Her passion has always been to develop creative and meaningful inclusion opportunities for all students with varying disabilities. This book continues her mission to *Empower Empathy* by encouraging children to embrace their differences while exploring their similarities.